100 AMAZING FACTS ABOUT PARIS

© 2023, Marc Dresgui

Content

Introduction 8

Fact 1 - Paris: First called Lutetia! 9

Fact 2 - Did the Vikings attack Paris? 10

Fact 3 - The Seine, the beating heart of Paris. 11

Fact 4 - The Eiffel Tower was not liked at first! 12

Fact 5 - Notre-Dame: More than 800 years of history. 13

Fact 6 - The Louvre: From a fortress to a museum 14

Fact 7 - The ghost of the Opera Garnier. 15

Fact 8 - The legend of the bloody baker. 16

Fact 9 - Napoleon: The emperor buried under gold. 17

Fact 10 - Marie-Antoinette and her last trip. 18

Fact 11 - The bustling markets of the Middle Ages. 19

Fact 12 - The masked balls of the 19th century. 20

Fact 13 - The first photograph taken in Paris. 21

Fact 14 - Cinema was born in Paris! 22

Fact 15 - Monet and the beginnings of Impressionism. 23

Fact 16 - The national holiday of July 14. 24

Fact 17 - The White Night: Paris awakens! 25

Fact 18 - The wolves that once haunted Paris. 26

Fact 19 - The Tuileries Garden: Royal Oasis. 27

Fact 20 - The mystery of the Sainte-Chapelle. 28

Fact 21 - La Tour Montparnasse: Love or hate? 29

Fact 22 - Montmartre: The artists' village. 30

Fact 23 - The Swamp: From swamps to fashion. 31

Fact 24 - The Paris metro: A world underground. 32

Fact 25 - Les bateaux-mouches: Flight over the Seine. 33

Fact 26 - The Paris of the Belle Époque. 34

Fact 27 - The covered passages: Secrets of the 19th. 35

Fact 28 - The guillotine: The revolutionary invention. 36

Fact 29 - The Catacombs: The Underground City. 37

Fact 30 - Picasso: A genius in Montmartre. 38

Fact 31 - New Year's fireworks. 39

Fact 32 - The animals of the Jardin des Plantes. 40

Fact 33 - The secrets of the Pont Neuf. 41

Fact 34 - The Sorbonne: The 800-year-old school. 42

Fact 35 - The sewers of Paris: A hidden world. 43

Fact 36 - Victor Hugo: The man behind "Les Misérables". 44

Fact 37 - La Fête de la Musique: All to dance! 45

Fact 38 - The historic trees of Paris. 46

Fact 39 - The mystery of the rue des Marmousets. 47

Fact 40 - La Défense : Futuristic and brilliant. 48

Fact 41 - Sainte-Geneviève: The protector of Paris. 49

Fact 42 - The artists of the Place du Tertre. 50

Fact 43 - The secrets of the Latin Quarter. 51

Fact 44 - The trams of yesteryear. 52

Fact 45 - The first wooden Eiffel Tower? 53

Fact 46 - The gargoyles of Notre-Dame. 54

Fact 47 - The coffee revolution in Paris. 55

Fact 48 - The historic chocolatiers of Paris. 56

Fact 49 - Parisian fashion through the ages. 57

Fact 50 - The ghosts of Père Lachaise. 58

Fact 51 - The Seine has frozen! 59

Fact 52 - The Moulin Rouge and its dancers. 60

Fact 53 - The secrets of the Pantheon. 61

Fact 54 - The inventions of the Universal Exhibition. 62

Fact 55 - Toulouse-Lautrec: Life in color. 63

Fact 56 - The Bastille: Before the revolution. 64

Fact 57 - The amusement parks of yesteryear. 65

Fact 58 - The animals of the Bois de Boulogne. 66

Fact 59 - The mystery of the rue de la Ferronnerie. 67

Fact 60 - Le Grand Palais : A glass jewel. 68

Fact 61 - La Rive Gauche: L'âme bohème. 69

Fact 62 - The secrets of Chinatown. 70

Fact 63 - The double-decker buses of Paris. 71

Fact 64 - The first floating bookstore. 72

Fact 65 - The statues that speak. 73

Fact 66 - The dancing fountains of Paris. 74

Fact 67 - The rebirth of the Canal Saint-Martin. 75

Fact 68 - The painters of the Seine. 76

Fact 69 - The first school for girls. 77

Fact 70 - The bonfires of St. John. 78

Fact 71 - The animals of the Vincennes Zoo............................79

Fact 72 - The mystery of the sundial..................................80

Fact 73 - La Butte-aux-Cailles: Secret village.....................81

Fact 74 - The secrets of the Quartier des Halles..................82

Fact 75 - The yellow taxis of war.......................................83

Fact 76 - The first public clock...84

Fact 77 - The musicïans of the metro.................................85

Fact 78 - The harvest festival of Montmartre.......................86

Fact 79 - The birds of the Parisian gardens........................87

Fact 80 - The mystery of the Conciergerie..........................88

Fact 81 - La Villette: Science and fun................................89

Fact 82 - La Rive Droite: Chic and elegant.........................90

Fact 83 - The secrets of the Belleville District...................91

Fact 84 - The historic bikes of Paris.................................92

Fact 85 - The first exhibition of modern art......................93

Fact 86 - Street festivals in Paris....................................94

Fact 87 - The animals of the Menagerie............................95

Fact 88 - The mystery of the rue des Chantres...................96

Fact 89 - The Mouzaïa district: Little treasure...................97

Fact 90 - The secrets of the Bercy district........................98

Fact 91 - The vintage cars of Paris..................................99

Fact 92 - The first Parisian radio station....................... 100

Fact 93 - The artists of the Pont des Arts...................... 101

Fact 94 - The festival of lights of Paris......................... 102

Fact 95 - The butterflies of the Jardin des Plantes. 103

Fact 96 - The Square des Missions-Étrangères. 104

Fact 97 - Le Quartier de Batignolles : Discreet charm. 105

Fact 98 - The secrets of the Quartier de la Chapelle 106

Fact 99 - The airships of Paris. 107

Fact 100 - The first children's bookstore. 108

Conclusion 109

Quiz 110

Answers 115

"Paris is the city where you discover how happy you are to be alive."

— Jean-Paul Sartre

Introduction

Paris, the City of Light, is much more than just a tourist destination. It is the cradle of revolutions, eternal love stories, artistic masterpieces and innovations that have changed the world. Every street corner, every cobblestone, every façade hides a story, a secret or an anecdote waiting to be revealed. While most people know the Eiffel Tower, Notre-Dame or the Louvre, there are so many other facets of this majestic city that remain in the shadows, unknown to the general public.

In "100 Amazing Facts About Paris", we will dive into these stories less told, but just as fascinating. From the mysterious origins of certain neighborhoods to surprising anecdotes about emblematic places, this book is an invitation to rediscover Paris in a new light. Whether you're a long-time resident, a newcomer, or just a lover of this city, prepare to be amazed.

Because Paris, with its thousand and one lives, never ceases to surprise, inspire and captivate. Let's embark together on a journey through the alleys, boulevards and centuries, to discover the hidden treasures of the French capital.

Marc Dresgui

Fact 1 - Paris: First called Lutetia!

Hi, dear reader! Did you know that long before Paris was called "Paris", it had another name? Yes, that's right! The City of Light that you know today had a very different name in antiquity: Lutetia.

Lutetia was a small island located on the Seine, where the Île de la Cité is today. It was the beating heart of the city in Gallo-Roman times. The Parisii, a Celtic tribe, were the first known inhabitants of this region. They gave the city its original name.

Over time, Lutetia grew and developed, becoming an important commercial and cultural center. Then, over the centuries, its name evolved to become "Paris", in honor of the Parisii tribe.

So, the next time you walk the streets of Paris, remember that you are walking in the footsteps of an ancient civilization, in a city that has a rich and fascinating history long before it was called Paris.

Fact 2 - Did the Vikings attack Paris?

Hey, budding adventurer! Have you ever heard of the Vikings, those fearsome warriors from the North? These men, famous for their horned helmets and drakkars, sailed many rivers and seas. But do you know if they have ever set foot in Paris?

The answer is yes! In 845, a large Viking army led by a leader named Ragnar Lothbrok sailed up the Seine. Their goal? Attack and plunder Paris. The Parisians, terrified, tried to defend their city, but the Vikings were numerous and well organized.

The king at the time, Charles the Bald, finally decided to pay a huge ransom to the Vikings to leave Paris without destroying it. This strategy worked, but the Vikings returned several times, attracted by the city's riches.

So, the next time you walk on the banks of the Seine, imagine these fierce Viking warriors sailing on their large ships, ready to launch an assault on the beautiful Lutetia!

Fact 3 - The Seine, the beating heart of Paris.

Hi, curious explorer! When you think of Paris, what are the first things that come to mind? The Eiffel Tower, the Louvre, perhaps? But have you ever thought about the Seine, the majestic river that runs through the city?

The Seine has always been the true heart of Paris. It has played a crucial role in the development of the city since its inception. Thanks to it, Paris became an important commercial center, as goods could be easily transported by river.

The many bridges that span the Seine, such as the Pont Neuf or the Pont des Arts, each tell a part of the history of Paris. They have witnessed dates, revolutions and celebrations.

So the next time you stand by the Seine, take a moment to admire its beauty and think about all the historical events it has seen over the centuries. It is much more than just a river; it is the soul of Paris.

Fact 4 - The Eiffel Tower was not liked at first!

Hey, architecture lover! The Eiffel Tower is undoubtedly the most emblematic symbol of Paris. But would you believe that when it was built, many Parisians did not like it at all?

Indeed, during its construction for the Universal Exhibition of 1889, many artists and intellectuals of the time criticized the tower. They considered it an "aberration" and thought it spoiled the Parisian landscape. Some have even called it "the iron skeleton"!

Gustave Eiffel, the engineer behind this feat, had to defend his project with passion. He believed in his vision and was convinced that the tower would become a masterpiece. And he was right! Over time, the criticism faded and the Eiffel Tower became one of the most loved and visited monuments in the world.

So the next time you look up to admire this magnificent structure, remember that it hasn't always been so popular. But today, it is the proud symbol of the City of Light!

Fact 5 - Notre-Dame: More than 800 years of history.

Hi, history buff! Have you ever visited Notre-Dame Cathedral in Paris? This Gothic masterpiece is one of the city's most famous landmarks. But do you know how many stories she lived?

Notre-Dame was built between the 12th and 14th centuries. Yes, you read that right! It took almost 200 years to complete this architectural marvel. Over the centuries, it has witnessed royal coronations, weddings and even state funerals.

But that's not all. Notre Dame has also survived wars, revolutions and fires, most recently in 2019, which moved the entire world. Despite these hardships, she remains standing, proud and majestic.

So, the next time you pass by this cathedral, think about all the stories it has lived. Each stone, each stained glass window tells a piece of the history of Paris. Notre-Dame is not only a monument, it is a book open to the past.

Fact 6 - The Louvre: From a fortress to a museum.

Cuckoo, art and history lover! The Louvre Museum is one of the largest museums in the world, housing treasures like the Mona Lisa. But did you know that the Louvre has not always been a museum?

Originally, in the 12th century, the Louvre was a fortress built to protect Paris from invasions. If you look closely, you can still see the remains of this ancient fortress in the foundations of the current museum.

Over the centuries, the Louvre has been transformed and expanded from a royal residence to a place dedicated to art and culture. It was in 1793, during the French Revolution, that it became a museum open to the public.

So the next time you wander through the Louvre's vast galleries, remember its rich past. Behind every work of art, there is a story, and the building itself has a fascinating saga to tell, ranging from medieval knights to Renaissance artists.

Fact 7 - The ghost of the Opera Garnier.

Hey, lover of mysteries! The Opéra Garnier is one of the most sumptuous buildings in Paris, with its gilding, mirrors and gleaming chandeliers. But have you heard of its most mysterious resident: the Phantom of the Opera?

Legend has it that a disfigured man, living in the underground of the Opera, fell in love with a young singer. Hidden in the shadows, he guided and protected her, while terrorizing those who stood in his way.

This story inspired many artists, including Gaston Leroux, who wrote the famous novel "The Phantom of the Opera" in 1910. Since then, the legend has been adapted into films, musicals and even ballets.

So, the next time you visit the Opera Garnier, listen. Who knows, maybe you'll hear the distant melodies of the ghost or the whisper of his footsteps in the dark corridors. After all, every great scene needs its mystery!

Fact 8 - The legend of the bloody baker.

Hi, thrill seekers! Paris is full of stories and legends, some more frightening than others. Have you ever heard of the terrifying legend of the bloody baker of the rue des Marmousets?

In the 14th century, a baker named Jean de la Barre would have had a very particular way of preparing his breads. According to legend, to take revenge on the thieves who tried to steal his merchandise, he killed them, then used their bodies as an ingredient for his loaves!

This macabre story has been circulating for years in the streets of Paris. Some say customers at the bakery became suspicious when bones and teeth were found in the loaves. Rumor has it that Jean and his wife were arrested and executed for their crimes.

So, the next time you walk the streets of Paris, think of all the legends behind every corner. And above all, choose your bakery well!

Fact 9 - Napoleon: The emperor buried under gold.

Hi, young historian! Napoleon Bonaparte is undoubtedly one of the most emblematic figures in French history. But do you know where this emperor who conquered a large part of Europe rests?

Napoleon is buried in Paris, under the magnificent golden dome of the Invalides. After his death in 1821 on the island of St. Helena, his body was brought back to France with full honours. In 1840, he was buried in an imposing sarcophagus of red porphyry, surrounded by laurels and inscriptions recalling his great victories.

The Invalides, with their brilliant gold dome, are visible from afar in the Parisian landscape. Inside, Napoleon's tomb is surrounded by great generals and military heroes, but it is he who occupies the central place.

So the next time you admire the golden dome of the Invalides, remember the powerful man who lies underneath. Napoleon, despite his controversies, remains a major figure in history, and his final resting place lives up to his legend.

Fact 10 - Marie-Antoinette and her last trip.

Hey, curious about the past! Marie Antoinette, the last queen of France before the Revolution, is a figure both adored and controversial. But do you know the story of his last trip through Paris?

Marie Antoinette was imprisoned in the Temple Tower after the fall of the monarchy. Accused of treason, she was sentenced to death. On October 16, 1793, she was taken to the Place de la Révolution (now Place de la Concorde) to be executed.

This journey, aboard a cart, was one of the most poignant moments of the Revolution. The Queen, despite her situation, remained dignified and courageous, accepting her fate with great strength of mind.

So, the next time you walk around the Place de la Concorde, think about this queen and her last journey. Behind the beauty and splendour of Paris lie stories of courage, tragedy and hope that shaped the city we know today.

Fact 11 - The bustling markets of the Middle Ages.

Hi, time traveler! Imagine, several centuries ago, in the heart of medieval Paris. The streets were animated by colorful and noisy markets. Do you want to know more about these places of life?

In the Middle Ages, markets were essential to everyday life. They were often held in the main squares of cities, and Paris was no exception. Merchants sold all kinds of products: fruits, vegetables, fish, spices and even fabrics from distant lands.

These markets were also places of meeting and exchange. They discussed the latest news, exchanged gossip, and negotiated prices fiercely. The shouts of the merchants, the laughter of the children and the lively discussions created a unique atmosphere.

So, the next time you walk through the streets of Paris, close your eyes and imagine the sounds, smells and colors of a medieval market. It's a journey back in time that will remind you how vibrant and lively the city has always been!

Fact 12 - The masked balls of the 19th century.

Hey, dancer at heart! Have you ever dreamed of participating in a masquerade ball, where everyone wears elegant costumes and mysterious masks? In the 19th century, Paris was the capital of these magical events!

Masked balls were very popular at that time. They were often held in large hotels or palaces, with orchestras playing lively music. Participants wore sumptuous costumes and masks, adding a touch of mystery to the evening.

These balls were an opportunity for high society to entertain, dance and flirt. But they were also a place where social classes mixed, because the mask allowed to hide one's identity and free oneself from conventions.

So the next time you hear a waltz or polka, imagine dancing in a large candlelit living room, surrounded by masked people. The masked balls of the 19th century reflected a time when elegance and mystery reigned supreme.

Fact 13 - The first photograph taken in Paris.

Hi, souvenir lover! Today, taking a photo is a daily gesture. But have you ever thought about the very first photograph taken in Paris? Let's dive into this fascinating story.

That was in 1838. A French inventor named Louis Daguerre, who gave his name to the daguerreotype, captured an image of the Rue du Temple in Paris. This photograph is considered the first photo of a person in an urban space.

If you look at this picture, you will see an almost empty street, except for a man having his shoes polished. Other passers-by are not visible because Daguerre's technique required long exposure, and only stationary objects were captured.

So, the next time you take a quick photo with your phone, think about that first image and the incredible evolution of photography. From long minutes of waiting to a fraction of a second, Paris has witnessed this visual revolution!

Fact 14 - Cinema was born in Paris!

Hey, budding movie buff! Do you love watching movies on the big screen? Did you know that cinema, this wonderful invention that allows us to travel in imaginary worlds, was born in Paris?

It all started with two brothers, Auguste and Louis Lumière. In 1895, they invented the cinematograph, a machine that could film and project moving images. Their first "cinema screening" took place at the Grand Café in Paris on December 28, 1895.

During this historic screening, the audience was amazed by simple scenes, such as a train arriving at the station or workers leaving a factory. These short sequences, while basic, marked the beginning of a new era of entertainment.

So, the next time you immerse yourself in a captivating movie, remember that this magic began in the busy streets of Paris. Thanks to the Lumière brothers, the City of Light has become the cradle of the 7th art!

Fact 15 - Monet and the beginnings of Impressionism.

Hi, art lovers! Have you ever been amazed by the bright colors and bold touches of paint in Impressionist paintings? Did you know that this revolutionary artistic movement took root in Paris?

Claude Monet, one of the pioneers of Impressionism, sought to capture the immediacy and changing light in his works. Instead of painting in the studio, he preferred to work outdoors to capture nature in all its glory.

In 1874, Monet exhibited one of his paintings entitled "Impression, rising sun". It is from this painting that the term "Impressionism" was born, first used mockingly by critics before being adopted by the artists themselves.

So, the next time you get lost in the nuances of an impressionist painting, remember Monet and his artist friends in Paris. They dared to defy convention and created a movement that continues to inspire and amaze the world.

Fact 16 - The national holiday of July 14.

Hi, history buff! Every year, on July 14, Paris lights up with fireworks and resonates to the sound of parades. But do you know why the French celebrate this date with such enthusiasm?

On July 14, 1789, the Bastille, a prison and symbol of the absolute power of the king, was stormed by the Parisian people. This event marked the beginning of the French Revolution, a period of great political and social upheaval.

Since then, July 14 has become France's national holiday, celebrating liberty, equality and fraternity. Every year, a large military parade takes place on the Champs-Élysées, followed by festivities and fireworks.

So, the next time you see the Parisian sky light up on July 14, remember the story behind that date. It is a celebration of freedom and democracy, values dear to the hearts of the French people.

Fact 17 - The White Night: Paris awakens!

Hey, curious night owl! Have you ever wandered the streets of Paris on a night when the city never sleeps? Every year, during the "Nuit Blanche", Paris comes alive in a very special way.

The Nuit Blanche is an artistic event that transforms Paris into a huge art gallery open all night. Installations, performances and light projections come to life in streets, parks and even some historic buildings.

This is a unique opportunity for Parisians and visitors to rediscover the city from a new angle. Artists from all over the world come to share their creations, making Paris a real artistic playground.

So, the next time you find yourself in Paris during the Nuit Blanche, let yourself be carried away by the magic of art and the night. It is a unique experience where the City of Light shines in a totally different way, awake and vibrant until the early hours.

Fact 18 - The wolves that once haunted Paris.

Hi, adventurer of urban legends! Paris, with its lights and animation, seems far from the wilderness. But did you know that there was a time when wolves roamed the streets of the capital?

In the Middle Ages, when Paris was still surrounded by forests and fields, wolves were common predators. During harsh winters, hunger sometimes drove these creatures into the city in search of food.

One of the most famous stories is that of the "louperie" of 1450. That year, a pack of hungry wolves entered Paris, spreading terror among the inhabitants. These wolves were hunted down and finally killed on the Place de Grève, the current Place de l'Hôtel de Ville.

So, the next time you walk the busy streets of Paris, imagine for a moment these wild creatures wandering the alleys. It is a fascinating reminder of the coexistence between man and nature, even in the heart of a large metropolis.

Fact 19 - The Tuileries Garden: Royal Oasis.

Hi, nature lovers! In the heart of Paris, between the Louvre and the Place de la Concorde, lies a magnificent garden. Do you know the history of the Tuileries Garden, this royal oasis in the middle of the urban hustle and bustle?

Created in the 16th century for Catherine de Medici, this garden was originally the park of a royal palace. With its tree-lined walkways, statues and ponds, it was the favorite place for kings and queens to relax and entertain.

Over the centuries, the Tuileries Garden has become a place open to all. Parisians and tourists come to walk there, enjoy the sun or simply admire the beauty of the landscape.

So, the next time you wander through this historic garden, think of the generations of royalty who once walked these same alleys. The Tuileries Garden is a true treasure of Paris, a bridge between royal history and modern city life.

Fact 20 - The mystery of the Sainte-Chapelle.

Hi, explorer of hidden wonders! In the heart of the Ile de la Cité, stands a chapel that seems straight out of a fairy tale. Have you ever heard of the mystery surrounding the Sainte-Chapelle?

Built in the 13th century by King Saint Louis, the Sainte-Chapelle was intended to house a precious relic: the Crown of Thorns of Christ. With its sparkling stained glass windows and celestial vault, it is considered a masterpiece of Gothic architecture.

But that's not all. Some say the chapel holds secrets. Legends speak of hidden passages and buried treasures, although nothing has ever been proven.

So, the next time you visit this wonder, let yourself be carried away by its mystical atmosphere. The Sainte-Chapelle is not only a place of worship, it is also a treasure set of mysteries and legends waiting to be discovered.

Fact 21 - La Tour Montparnasse: Love or hate?

Hi, urban explorer! When you look at the Paris skyline, one building stands out from the rest. Have you ever noticed the Montparnasse Tower, this huge black tower that dominates the city?

Built in the 1970s, the Montparnasse Tower is the tallest skyscraper in Paris. With its 210 meters high, it offers a breathtaking panoramic view of the capital. From its summit, you can see all the emblematic monuments of Paris!

However, despite its exceptional view, the tower has often been criticized for its modern design and contrasts with the Haussmann landscape of Paris. Some love it, some hate it. It is even sometimes nicknamed the "pencil box" because of its shape.

So, the next time you look up at the Montparnasse Tower, ask yourself what you think. Is it an architectural abomination or a bold symbol of modernity? In Paris, each building has its own story and arouses different emotions!

Fact 22 - Montmartre: The artists' village.

Hi, creative soul! Have you ever climbed the steps that lead to Montmartre, the hill overlooking Paris? This place is much more than just a neighborhood: it has been the refuge of artists for generations.

In the 19th and early 20th centuries, Montmartre was a real village away from the hustle and bustle of Paris. With its winding streets and artists' studios, it attracted painters, writers and musicians. Famous names such as Picasso, Van Gogh or Toulouse-Lautrec found inspiration here.

The Place du Tertre, in the heart of Montmartre, is always animated by artists who paint portraits or exhibit their works. It is a place where art is alive, palpable, on every street corner.

So, the next time you walk through the streets of Montmartre, feel the creative energy that reigns there. Imagine the artists of yesteryear, working on their masterpieces, and let yourself be inspired by this unique atmosphere. Montmartre is a living testimony to the artistic passion of Paris.

Fact 23 - The Swamp: From swamps to fashion.

Hi, explorer of the Parisian neighborhoods! Have you ever strolled through the narrow, cobbled streets of the Marais? This historic district of Paris has a fascinating history that dates back centuries.

Originally, the Marais was literally a "swamp", a wetland and swamp. But over time, it has become one of the most sought-after areas of Paris, home to magnificent mansions and secret squares.

In the 17th century, the Parisian nobility began to build sumptuous residences in the Marais. Today, these historic buildings house museums, art galleries and chic boutiques.

So the next time you walk around the Marais, think about its evolution from swamps to a center of fashion and culture. Every stone, every alley, tells a story of transformation and renewal. This is the essence of Paris: a city that evolves while cherishing its rich past.

Fact 24 - The Paris metro: A world underground.

Hi, adventurer of the deep! When you travel to Paris, do you take the metro, this underground network that winds under the city? Let's dive together into the history of this labyrinth under the cobblestones.

Inaugurated in 1900, the Paris metro was designed to facilitate travel in a booming city. With its entrances adorned with beautiful Art Nouveau ironwork, it quickly became emblematic of Paris.

Today, the metro has more than 200 km of tracks and serves hundreds of stations. Every day, millions of Parisians and tourists use it, making it one of the busiest metros in the world.

So the next time you walk down the stairs to a station, imagine all the technical challenges and engineering feats required to create this world underground. The Paris metro is much more than just a means of transport: it is a real architectural feat and a witness to the history of Paris.

Fact 25 - Les bateaux-mouches: Flight over the Seine.

Hi, lovers of the waves! Have you ever sailed on the Seine, admiring Paris from a riverboat? These iconic boats offer a unique perspective on the City of Light.

The history of riverboats dates back to the 19th century. They take their name from the "Mouche", a district of Lyon where the first boats of this type were built. These ships were originally intended for the transport of goods.

But very quickly, their vocation changed. Parisians and tourists alike began using them for river cruises, admiring the capital's iconic landmarks from the water. Today, a boat trip is a must for any visitor to Paris.

So, the next time you stand on the deck of a riverboat, let yourself be carried away by the charm of Paris. From the Eiffel Tower to Notre-Dame, each monument is reflected in the waters of the Seine, offering an unforgettable spectacle. Embark on an adventure along the water!

Fact 26 - The Paris of the Belle Époque.

Hi, time traveler! Have you ever dreamed of walking around Paris in the late 19th and early 20th centuries? It was the time of the "Belle Époque", a time of peace, prosperity and innovation.

During these years, Paris underwent a spectacular transformation. Grand boulevards were laid out, monuments like the Eiffel Tower were erected, and World Expos attracted visitors from all over the world.

Culture has also flourished. Cabarets, such as the Moulin Rouge, were born, and artists such as Toulouse-Lautrec captured the spirit of the time in their works. It was a time of artistic effervescence and discovery.

So, the next time you walk around Paris, imagine the bustling streets of the Belle Époque, with its elegant ladies in long dresses and gentlemen in top hats. It was a time when Paris shone, capturing the imagination of all who visited it.

Fact 27 - The covered passages: Secrets of the 19th.

Hi, explorer of hidden treasures! Have you ever wandered through the covered passages of Paris? These elegant galleries, true precursors of modern shopping centers, are windows into the 19th century.

Born in the early 19th century, these passages were havens for shopping and entertainment. With their mosaic floors, glass roofs and fine shops, they offered Parisians shelter from the weather while shopping.

Each passage has its own personality. Some, like the Passage des Panoramas, were famous for their theaters and shows. Others, such as the Passage Jouffroy, were renowned for their bookstores and antique shops.

So the next time you find yourself in one of these passages, take a moment to immerse yourself in the atmosphere of the 19th century. It is a journey back in time, to a time when Paris was in full mutation and when these passages were the beating heart of urban life.

Fact 28 - The guillotine: The revolutionary invention.

Hi, curious about history! Have you ever heard of the guillotine, this machine that is both fascinating and terrifying? It became the symbol of the French Revolution, but do you know its history?

The guillotine was invented with the aim of being a "humane" means of execution, fast and painless. Its name comes from Dr. Joseph-Ignace Guillotin, who proposed its use, although he is not the inventor.

During the French Revolution, it became the instrument of revolutionary "justice". In public squares such as the Place de la Concorde, important figures, from Marie-Antoinette to Robespierre, met their end under his sharp blade.

So the next time you hear about the guillotine, remember its role in France's story. It is a reflection of a tumultuous time, when the ideals of freedom and equality were confronted with the brutal reality of revolution.

Fact 29 - The Catacombs: The Underground City.

Hi, adventurer of the deep! Do you have the courage to explore the bowels of Paris? Beneath the busy streets lie the catacombs, a labyrinth of tunnels filled with bones.

Originally, these tunnels were quarries, used to extract the stone that was used to build Paris. But in the 18th century, faced with the congestion of cemeteries, a solution was found: transfer the bones to these underground.

Today, a small part of the catacombs is open to the public. Going down the stairs, you will find yourself facing walls of bones, carefully arranged. It's both strange and fascinating, a reminder of the fragility of life.

So the next time you walk the streets of Paris, think about what's under your feet. The catacombs are a silent testimony to the history of the city, an underground world where the past rests in peace.

Fact 30 - Picasso: A genius in Montmartre.

Hi, art lover! Have you ever dreamed of following in the footsteps of one of the greatest artists of the 20th century? Pablo Picasso, the master of cubism, left his mark in Montmartre.

As a young artist, Picasso settled in Montmartre at the beginning of the 20th century. In his workshop at the "Bateau-Lavoir", he experimented, innovated and created works that would revolutionize the art world.

It was in Montmartre that he painted one of his most famous works, "Les Demoiselles d'Avignon". This bold canvas laid the foundation for Cubism, an artistic movement that changed the way we perceive the world.

So, the next time you walk through the streets of Montmartre, think about Picasso and his creative genius. Imagine him, painting feverishly in his studio, driven by an insatiable passion for art. Montmartre was not only his home, it was his muse.

Fact 31 - New Year's fireworks.

Hi, lover of twinkling lights! Have you ever experienced the passage to the new year in Paris? The French capital lights up with a thousand lights to celebrate this special occasion.

Every December 31, as midnight approaches, thousands of people gather around the Eiffel Tower and other iconic places. The anticipation is palpable, everyone waiting for the upcoming show.

At exactly midnight, the sky goes up in flames. Fireworks erupt, illuminating the Parisian night with bright colors and sparkling patterns. The Eiffel Tower, already majestic, becomes the center of a breathtaking light show.

So, the next time you have the opportunity to celebrate New Year's Eve in Paris, prepare to be amazed. It is a time of joy, renewal and hope, and Paris celebrates it with unparalleled beauty and grandeur.

Fact 32 - The animals of the Jardin des Plantes.

Hi, nature lovers! Have you ever visited the Jardin des Plantes in Paris? This haven of greenery in the heart of the city is home to a fascinating menagerie of animals.

Since its creation in the 17th century, the Jardin des Plantes has always had the vocation to educate and amaze. Over the years, a menagerie has been established, welcoming animals from all over the world.

In this menagerie, you can meet creatures as varied as kangaroos, reptiles or exotic birds. Each enclosure is designed to provide a suitable habitat for its residents, while allowing visitors to observe them up close.

So, next time you walk through the Jardin des Plantes, take a moment to visit the menagerie. It is a unique opportunity to discover rare and fascinating animals, while learning about the biodiversity of our planet. An adventure in the heart of nature, in the heart of Paris!

Fact 33 - The secrets of the Pont Neuf.

Hi, explorer of the streets of Paris! Have you ever crossed the Pont Neuf, this emblematic bridge that spans the Seine? Despite its name, it is actually the oldest bridge in Paris.

Built in the late 16th century, the Pont Neuf was the first bridge in Paris without houses built on it. With its stone arches and carved heads, it has become a symbol of the city.

But did you know that he hides secrets? Under its arches, small niches were once used by traders. And the famous carved heads, called "mascarons", represent the faces of Parisians of the time!

So, the next time you walk on the Pont Neuf, look at it with a fresh eye. Imagine merchants selling their wares, artists capturing scenes of everyday life, and Parisians from all walks of life crossing this historic bridge. Each stone, each sculpture, tells a story.

Fact 34 - The Sorbonne: The 800-year-old school.

Hi, curious about historical places! Have you ever heard of the Sorbonne, this prestigious institution nestled in the heart of the Latin Quarter? It is one of the oldest universities in the world.

Founded in 1257 by Robert de Sorbon, a chaplain to King Saint Louis, the Sorbonne was originally a simple school for poor students. It quickly became a centre of excellence, attracting brilliant minds from all over Europe.

Over the centuries, the Sorbonne has trained generations of thinkers, writers and leaders. Illustrious names such as René Descartes or Simone de Beauvoir have walked its corridors, enriching the intellectual heritage of the France.

So, the next time you pass by the Sorbonne, think about all the knowledge that has been shared within its walls. It is a place where history, culture and knowledge have intertwined for nearly 800 years, making Paris a beacon of global education.

Fact 35 - The sewers of Paris: A hidden world.

Hi, adventurer of the deep! Have you ever imagined what lies beneath the cobbled streets of Paris? An intricate system of sewers winds beneath the city, testifying to human ingenuity.

Since the 13th century, Paris has developed its sewers to manage wastewater and prevent flooding. But it wasn't until the 19th century, during the reign of Napoleon III, that the current system really took shape.

These underground tunnels are not only used for water disposal. They have also been the scene of fascinating stories! From workers to sewers, to novelists like Victor Hugo, many have been inspired by this labyrinth.

So, the next time you walk in Paris, think about this world hidden under your feet. If you're really curious, there are even guided tours of the sewers! It is a dive into history and engineering, in the heart of underground Paris.

Fact 36 - Victor Hugo: The man behind "Les Misérables".

Hi, literature lovers! Have you ever immersed yourself in the world of "Les Misérables", this epic masterpiece? Its author, Victor Hugo, is one of the most emblematic literary figures of Paris.

Born in 1802, Hugo grew up in a rapidly changing France. Poet, playwright and novelist, he used his pen to denounce the social and political injustices of his time. "Les Misérables" is undoubtedly his most famous work, telling the crossed destinies of unforgettable characters like Jean Valjean or Cosette.

Victor Hugo was not only a writer. He was also a committed man, fighting for causes such as the abolition of the death penalty. His house, Place des Vosges, is now a museum where you can discover his life and work.

So, the next time you read "Les Misérables" or walk near the Place des Vosges, think of Victor Hugo. He was a man who believed deeply in the ability of literature to change the world.

Fact 37 - La Fête de la Musique: All to dance!

Hi, budding music lover! Have you ever felt the energy of Paris during the Fête de la Musique? Every June 21st, the city comes alive to the rhythm of melodies from all walks of life.

The idea of this festival was born in 1982, under the impetus of the Minister of Culture at the time, Jack Lang. The concept? Encourage everyone, amateur or professional musicians, to take to the streets and share their passion for music.

From rock to jazz, classical music or electro, there is something for everyone. The streets, the parks, the terraces... every corner of Paris becomes an improvised stage where talents are revealed.

So the next time you're in Paris on June 21st, get ready to dance and sing until the end of the night. The Fête de la Musique is a celebration of diversity, creativity and, above all, the unifying power of music.

Fact 38 - The historic trees of Paris.

Hi, nature lovers! Did you know that some trees in Paris have seen centuries of history? These silent giants are living witnesses to the city's past.

In the heart of Square René-Viviani, you can admire the oldest tree in Paris. Planted in 1601, this locust tree has seen kings, revolutions and eras pass. Imagine what he could say if he could talk!

In the Jardin des Plantes, a cedar of Lebanon planted in 1734 sits majestically. It was introduced in France by botanist Bernard de Jussieu and is one of the first of its kind to be planted in Europe.

But they are not the only ones! Paris is full of remarkable trees, each with its own history. Some were planted in honor of great events, others survived wars or natural disasters.

So, next time you're walking around Paris, take a moment to admire these historic trees. They are the living link between the past and the present, anchoring the city in a natural and historical continuity.

Fact 39 - The mystery of the rue des Marmousets.

Hi, budding detective! Have you ever heard of the mysterious rue des Marmousets, nestled in the 4th arrondissement of Paris? This small street hides a dark and fascinating history.

In the Middle Ages, this street was known for a strange house. At his window, statues of monkeys (or "marmousets" in Old French) seemed to offer food to passers-by. But beware, everything was not so innocent!

It is said that the owner of this house used these statues to attract passers-by. Once inside, they mysteriously disappeared. Some say they were robbed, others said they were victims of more sinister acts.

Although this story is probably a legend, it gave its name to the street. Today, the rue des Marmousets is peaceful, but its mysterious past continues to fascinate.

So, the next time you walk in the Marais, think about this legend. Rue des Marmousets is a reminder that behind every corner of Paris, there can be a story to discover.

Fact 40 - La Défense : Futuristic and brilliant.

Hi, modern-day explorer! Have you ever looked up at the gleaming skyscrapers of La Défense? This business district is like a leap into the future, in the heart of the Paris region.

La Défense was born in the 1960s with a bold vision: to create a modern and innovative business centre. Today, it is the largest business district in Europe, with its glass and steel towers scratching the sky.

But it's not just offices! La Défense is also famous for its art. As you walk, you'll discover modern sculptures, fountains and the iconic Grande Arche, which aligns perfectly with the Arc de Triomphe if you look from the Avenue de la Grande Armée.

So, the next time you visit Paris, don't forget to make a detour to La Défense. It is a unique experience, where the historical past of Paris meets the bright and bold future. A perfect fusion between history and modernity.

Fact 41 - Sainte-Geneviève: The protector of Paris.

Hi, passionate about inspiring stories! Do you know the story of Sainte-Geneviève, this courageous woman who became the protector of Paris? His dedication left an indelible mark on the city.

Born in the 5th century, Geneviève was a pious young girl. When the Huns threatened to invade Paris, she encouraged residents to stay and pray rather than flee. Thanks to his unwavering faith, it is said, the city was spared.

In recognition of his courage, a church was built in his honour on Montagne Sainte-Geneviève. Today, it is the famous Pantheon, where great names in French history are buried.

So, the next time you walk in the Latin Quarter, think of Sainte-Geneviève. His determination and faith not only saved Paris from invasion, but also inspired generations of Parisians. It is a symbol of resilience and hope for the City of Light.

Fact 42 - The artists of the Place du Tertre.

Hi, art and culture lover! Have you ever strolled through the Place du Tertre in Montmartre? This picturesque little square has been the beating heart of Parisian artistic life for decades.

At the beginning of the 20th century, Montmartre was the haunt of artists. Picasso, Modigliani, Utrillo... All were inspired by the unique atmosphere of this neighborhood. The Place du Tertre, with its cobblestones and terraces, was their playground.

Today, the tradition continues. Artists gather every day in this square to paint, draw and capture the essence of Paris. With a little luck, you could even leave with a portrait of yourself, sketched in a few minutes!

So, next time you visit Montmartre, take the time to stop at the Place du Tertre. Let yourself be carried away by the artistic atmosphere, the bright colors and the incredible talents that are revealed there. It is a real journey back in time, to the heart of the artistic soul of Paris.

Fact 43 - The secrets of the Latin Quarter.

Hi, urban adventurer! Have you ever explored the winding alleys of the Latin Quarter? This historic corner of Paris is full of secrets and stories just waiting to be discovered.

The name "Latin Quarter" comes from Latin, the language once spoken by students at the Sorbonne, one of the oldest universities in the world. Yes, this is where brilliant minds have studied for centuries!

But that's not all. As you wander, you will discover old bookstores, literary cafes and hidden theaters. Each stone seems to whisper stories of the past, from passionate debates to student revolutions.

So, on your next Paris getaway, immerse yourself in the Latin Quarter. Whether it's to find an old book, enjoy a coffee on the terrace or simply get lost in its streets steeped in history, this neighborhood has some nice surprises in store for you. It is a journey through time, to the heart of the Parisian intellect.

Fact 44 - The trams of yesteryear.

Hi, curious traveler! Did you know that long before buses and the metro, Parisians traveled by tram? These vehicles, drawn by horses, were the kings of the Parisian streets at the end of the 19th century.

The first trams appeared in Paris in the 1850s. They were made of wood, open and pulled by one or more horses. Imagine walking along the grand boulevards aboard these trams, with the sound of hooves echoing on the cobblestones!

But with the arrival of electricity, trams have evolved. In the 1900s, electric trams began to crisscross the city, faster and more modern. They were the preferred means of transport for many Parisians.

However, with the development of the metro and buses, trams gradually disappeared in the 1930s. But don't worry! Today, the tramway is making a comeback in Paris, in a modern form, to help relieve congestion in the city. A beautiful history lesson that shows that sometimes, the past can inspire the future!

Fact 45 - The first wooden Eiffel Tower?

Hi, lover of surprising anecdotes! Have you ever heard that the Eiffel Tower has a little wooden sister? It's an incredible story, but true, that preceded the construction of our famous Iron Lady.

Before building the iron Eiffel Tower, Gustave Eiffel and his team wanted to be sure of their project. For this, they first created a wooden model, on a reduced scale, to visualize the final result.

This model, although much smaller than the actual Eiffel Tower, was impressive. It was exhibited in various places in Paris, allowing Parisians to familiarize themselves with this bold and avant-garde project.

Of course, this wooden version was only temporary. Once everything was approved, the construction of the real Eiffel Tower began, and it was inaugurated in 1889 for the Universal Exhibition.

So, the next time you admire the Eiffel Tower, remember its little wooden sister. It's a fascinating reminder that behind every great achievement, there is always a first step, a first try, before the final triumph.

Fact 46 - The gargoyles of Notre-Dame.

Hi, explorer of the mysteries! When you look up at Notre Dame Cathedral, did you notice those strange stone creatures that seem to watch over Paris? These are the gargoyles, and they have a fascinating story to tell.

Gargoyles are not only decorative. Originally, they had a very specific function: to evacuate rainwater away from the walls of the cathedral. Thanks to them, the water did not flow directly on the walls, thus preserving the stone.

But over time, these simple gutters have taken on fantastic shapes. Dragons, chimeras, monsters... Each gargoyle is unique and seems to tell its own story. Some say they protect the cathedral from evil spirits.

Next time you visit Notre Dame, take a moment to admire these stone guardians. They are the testimony of the genius of the craftsmen of the Middle Ages, who knew how to combine functionality and aesthetics. These mysterious creatures are a reminder of the rich and complex history of this magnificent cathedral.

Fact 47 - The coffee revolution in Paris.

Hi, lover of sweet treats! Did you know that coffee, the drink that so many Parisians love, has a rich and eventful history in the capital? Let's dive into this aromatic adventure together.

Coffee arrived in Paris in the 17th century, imported from distant eastern lands. At first, it was considered an exotic drink, tasted in special "cafes", the ancestors of our current cafes.

Quickly, these establishments became places of meeting and exchange. Philosophers, writers, artists... Everyone gathered around a cup to discuss, debate and share ideas. Coffee stimulated the mind and conversation!

Today, the tradition continues. The Parisian terraces are the scene of a thousand and one stories, where coffee always plays a central role. So, the next time you enjoy an espresso while watching Parisian life, remember the rich history of this drink. It is a journey through time, to the heart of Parisian culture.

Fact 48 - The historic chocolatiers of Paris.

Hi, curious gourmand! If you're a chocolate fan, you've come to the right place. Paris is famous for its chocolatiers who, over the centuries, have delighted the taste buds of the finest gourmets.

Chocolate arrived in Paris in the 17th century, from the Americas. At first, it was consumed as a hot drink, highly prized by the nobility. Imagine a thick hot chocolate, flavored with exotic spices!

Over time, Parisian artisans have perfected the art of chocolate, creating pralines, truffles and other delicacies. Some chocolatiers, such as Debauve & Welsh, have existed for over 200 years and have served kings and queens!

Today, a stroll through the streets of Paris will allow you to discover historic shops, where know-how is passed down from generation to generation. Each bite is a taste journey, mixing tradition and innovation.

So, during your next Parisian getaway, don't forget to stop by one of these shops. Parisian chocolate is an experience not to be missed, a real treasure for the taste buds!

Fact 49 - Parisian fashion through the ages.

Hi, passionate about elegance! Have you ever noticed that Paris is often called the "capital of fashion"? Let's dive into history together to discover why this city has been at the heart of trends for centuries.

As early as the 17th century, the Paris-based royal court of France dictated European fashion trends. Kings and queens, with their sumptuous outfits, inspired the elites of the continent. Imagine basket dresses, powdered wigs and red heels!

In the 19th century, haute couture was born in Paris. Houses like Worth and Lanvin opened their doors, creating tailor-made clothing for high society. It was the beginning of a fashion revolution!

Today, Paris hosts the biggest fashion shows, attracting designers, models and fashionistas from all over the world. The streets of the city are a real daily parade, where each Parisian expresses his or her unique style.

So, the next time you walk around Paris, observe the outfits around you. Each garment tells a story, a legacy of centuries of innovation and creativity in the fashion world.

Fact 50 - The ghosts of Père Lachaise.

Hi, adventurer of the unknown! Have you ever heard of the Père Lachaise cemetery in Paris? It is the largest cemetery in the city, and some say it is haunted. Do you dare to discover its mysteries?

Opened at the beginning of the 19th century, Père Lachaise is the final resting place of many celebrities, such as Jim Morrison, Édith Piaf and Oscar Wilde. With its winding alleys and ancient tombs, the atmosphere is unique.

But beyond its history, legends circulate. Some visitors report seeing shadows or hearing murmurs between the graves. Stories of strange encounters and inexplicable sensations abound.

Of course, it is likely that these stories are fueled by the mystical atmosphere of the place. But who knows? Perhaps on your next visit, you will feel the presence of these spirits from the past. So, keep an open mind and let yourself be carried away by the enchanting atmosphere of Père Lachaise. Who knows what you might discover?

Fact 51 - The Seine has frozen!

Hi, explorer of natural phenomena! Did you know that there were moments in history when the Seine, the river that runs through Paris, froze completely? Imagine walking on a thick layer of ice in the heart of the city!

The Seine froze several times, but one of the most memorable episodes occurred in 1709. That year, the winter was so harsh that the river turned into a natural skating rink. Parisians ventured onto the ice, organizing markets and parties.

Another notable frost occurred in 1879. The locals then built temporary cabins on the ice and even organized horse races! It was a real winter party in the heart of Paris.

Of course, such events are rare nowadays due to global warming. But they remain engraved in the collective memory. So, the next time you walk along the Seine, imagine this landscape transformed by ice and the joy of Parisians having fun on this frozen expanse.

Fact 52 - The Moulin Rouge and its dancers.

Hi, lover of dazzling shows! Have you ever heard of the Moulin Rouge? This is one of the most famous cabarets in the world, nestled in the heart of Montmartre in Paris. Ready for a trip back in time?

The Moulin Rouge opened its doors in 1889, at a time when Paris was in artistic effervescence. Quickly, it became the meeting place for artists, writers and celebrities. Imagine twinkling lights, feathers and glitter everywhere!

What really made this cabaret famous was the cancan. A bold and energetic dance performed by dancers in twirling skirts. These women, with their daring moves, captivated the audience and made the Moulin Rouge a symbol of Parisian nightlife.

Today, the Moulin Rouge continues to enchant its visitors with sumptuous shows and breathtaking performances. If you have the opportunity to visit, prepare to be amazed by the history, music and dance of this iconic place. It's an unmissable Parisian experience!

Fact 53 - The secrets of the Pantheon.

Hi, curious about great monuments! Do you know the Pantheon, this imposing structure that dominates the Latin Quarter of Paris? It is much more than just a building. Let's discover his secrets together!

Originally, the Pantheon was a church dedicated to Sainte-Geneviève, the patron saint of Paris. But over time, his vocation changed. Today, it is a mausoleum where the great men and women who marked the history of France rest.

Inside, you would be amazed by its magnificent architecture. But what is really fascinating is the underground crypt. This is where personalities like Voltaire, Rousseau, Victor Hugo and Marie Curie are buried. Each grave tells a story of genius, courage or dedication.

But the Pantheon also has its mysteries. Have you ever heard of Foucault's pendulum? It is a scientific experiment that was carried out for the first time in this building to prove the rotation of the Earth.

Next time you walk around Paris, don't forget to visit the Pantheon. It is a place where history, science and art meet, offering a unique and memorable experience.

Fact 54 - The inventions of the Universal Exhibition.

Hi, young aspiring inventor! Have you ever heard of the Universal Exhibitions in Paris? These great events were the scene of discoveries and inventions that changed the world. Ready to be amazed?

One of the most famous World Expos took place in 1889. It was on this occasion that the Eiffel Tower was built! Yes, this iconic symbol of Paris was actually an entry to the exhibition. Who would have thought?

But that's not all! In 1900, at another World's Fair, the first escalator was presented to the public. Imagine the surprise of visitors when they discovered this invention that seemed straight out of the future!

These exhibitions were not only showcases for new technologies. They were also places of cultural sharing, where countries from all over the world came to present their arts, traditions and innovations.

So the next time you use an escalator or admire the Eiffel Tower, remember the World Expos. They were truly magical moments of innovation and discovery in Paris!

Fact 55 - Toulouse-Lautrec: Life in color.

Hi, art and color lovers! Have you ever come across works by Henri de Toulouse-Lautrec? This fascinating painter captured the essence of Parisian life in the Belle Époque like no one else. Let's dive into its colorful world!

Born into an aristocratic family, Toulouse-Lautrec chose to live in the heart of Montmartre, the bohemian district of Paris. There, he witnessed the lively nights, cabarets and colorful characters.

He is best known for his posters of the Moulin Rouge. Thanks to him, dancers like La Goulue have become icons. His works depict nightlife with a touch of humor and great sensitivity.

Despite his short life, Toulouse-Lautrec left an indelible mark on art. His paintings are a vibrant testimony to Parisian life at a time when the city was the center of the artistic world.

The next time you visit a museum or gallery, keep an eye out for Toulouse-Lautrec's works. They will transport you to a lively Paris, full of music, dance and, of course, color!

Fact 56 - The Bastille: Before the revolution.

Hi, explorer of time! When we talk about the Bastille, you probably think of the French Revolution, don't you? But do you know what the Bastille was like before these tumultuous events? Let's discover his story together!

The Bastille, before being the symbol of the Revolution, was a fortress. Built in the 14th century, it was intended to protect Paris from English attacks during the Hundred Years War. Impressive, right?

Over time, the Bastille lost its military role. It became a state prison where those who displeased the king were imprisoned. Not very welcoming as a place, huh?

But on July 14, 1789, everything changed. The storming of the Bastille marked the beginning of the French Revolution. The fortress, a symbol of royal oppression, was destroyed by the Parisian people.

Today, nothing remains of the original Bastille. But every time you pass by the Place de la Bastille in Paris, remember its rich and complex history, long before the days of the Revolution.

Fact 57 - The amusement parks of yesteryear.

Hi, adventurer of times past! Today, amusement parks are often associated with places like Disneyland. But did you know that Paris had its own amusement parks long before Mickey and his friends? Let's embark on a journey back in time!

In the 19th century, the "Tivoli Garden" was the place to be. Located near the current Saint-Lazare train station, this park offered roller coasters, swings and even fireworks. Imagine, at the time, it was a great novelty!

Another magical place was the "Prater de Paris". Inspired by a famous Viennese park, it offered sensational attractions, shows and concerts. Parisians loved to meet there for fun.

Unfortunately, over time, these parks disappeared, replaced by buildings or other structures. But their festive and innovative spirit has left an indelible mark on the city.

The next time you walk around Paris, try to imagine the laughter and shouts of joy of visitors to these parks of yesteryear. The magic is always there, you just have to know where to look!

Fact 58 - The animals of the Bois de Boulogne.

Hey, nature lovers! If you walk around Paris, you probably know the Bois de Boulogne, this large green space to the west of the city. But did you know that it is home to a multitude of animals? Let's meet them!

The Bois de Boulogne is not only a place for humans to walk. It is also a refuge for many birds, such as ducks, swans and even some herons lounging near lakes. Open your eyes and you could see them!

But that's not all! If you walk around early in the morning or at nightfall, you might come across squirrels, rabbits and even, if you're very lucky, foxes that have taken up residence in the woods.

In addition to wildlife, the Bois de Boulogne is also home to the Jardin d'Acclimatation. There you can discover farm animals and some exotic species.

So, the next time you visit this beautiful green space, don't forget to greet its feathered and furry inhabitants. They are an integral part of the magic of the place!

Fact 59 - The mystery of the rue de la Ferronnerie.

Hi, budding detective! Have you ever heard of the rue de la Ferronnerie, located in the 1st arrondissement of Paris? It hides a historical secret that I will reveal to you. Ready for a dive into the past?

This street, now animated by merchants and passers-by, was the scene of a tragic event in 1610. It was here that King Henry IV, nicknamed the "Vert-Galant", was assassinated in his carriage by a fanatic named Ravaillac.

If you look closely, you will see a commemorative plaque and some cobblestones carved on the ground, marking the exact spot where the king was attacked. It is a silent reminder of this event that changed the course of French history.

Henry IV was a beloved king for his peace efforts and religious tolerance. His death deeply marked the people of Paris. So next time you walk down this street, take a moment to remember this king and his legacy. Every corner of Paris has a story to tell!

Fact 60 - Le Grand Palais : A glass jewel.

Hi, urban explorer! Have you ever looked up at the Grand Palais during your Parisian walks? This monument is a true architectural marvel, and I will reveal some of its secrets.

Built for the Universal Exhibition of 1900, the Grand Palais is a masterpiece of art nouveau. With its gigantic glass roof, it is often compared to a "cathedral of glass and steel". Imagine: this canopy is one of the largest in the world!

Inside, the Grand Palais has hosted many events, from art exhibitions to fashion shows. It is a place where art, culture and history meet, always offering something new to discover.

But that's not all! The Grand Palais is also famous for its temporary exhibitions that attract visitors from all over the world. So, next time you're in Paris, don't forget to visit this glass and steel gem. You will be amazed by its beauty and history!

Fact 61 - La Rive Gauche: L'âme bohème.

Hey, adventurer of history! Have you ever strolled on the Left Bank in Paris? It is a place where art, literature and bohemia have always been in the spotlight. Let me tell you about its unique charm.

The Left Bank is the southern part of the Seine, and it has always been the haunt of artists, writers and intellectuals. Famous names like Hemingway, Picasso or Sartre frequented its cafes and bookstores. Imagine sitting on a terrace, inspired by the same atmosphere!

Neighborhoods like Saint-Germain-des-Prés and the Latin Quarter are emblematic of this Left Bank. They breathe culture, with their small cobbled streets, typical bistros and independent shops.

But that's not all! The Left Bank is also an atmosphere, a state of mind. It is the place for reflection, passionate discussion and creativity. So, on your next visit to Paris, take the time to get lost in its alleys and feel the bohemian soul that reigns there. You won't regret it!

Fact 62 - The secrets of Chinatown.

Hi, curious explorer! Have you ever heard of Paris' Chinatown? Located mainly in the 13th arrondissement, it is a vibrant place of culture and traditions. Ready for an Asian getaway in the heart of Paris?

Chinatown is the largest in Europe! As you walk around, you can admire pagodas, Asian supermarkets and even traditional massage parlors. It's like a little trip to Asia without leaving Paris.

But this neighborhood is not only Chinese. It is also home to many other Asian communities, such as Vietnamese, Laotians and Cambodians. Every year, Chinese New Year is celebrated here with parades, dragons and firecrackers. A party not to be missed!

Behind its bustling streets, Chinatown also hides fascinating stories. Did you know that it was built in the 1970s and that it played a key role for Asian immigrants in France? Next time you visit Paris, don't forget to immerse yourself in the mysteries of this unique neighborhood!

Fact 63 - The double-decker buses of Paris.

Hey, urban adventurer! When you think of double-decker buses, London probably comes to mind with its famous red buses. But did you know that Paris also had its own double-decker buses?

These buses, called "imperial", appeared in Paris in the 19th century. At the time, they were drawn by horses. Imagine walking through the cobbled streets of Paris aboard these giants, with the wind in your hair on the upper floor!

However, with the arrival of trams and motorized buses, double-decker buses gradually disappeared from the streets of Paris in the early 20th century. It is only recently, with the rise of tourism, that they have made their comeback, mainly for tourist tours.

Today, these buses offer a breathtaking view of the emblematic monuments of Paris. If you have the opportunity, get on board and discover the City of Light from a high perspective. It's an experience you won't soon forget!

Fact 64 - The first floating bookstore.

Hi, lover of curiosities! When you walk along the Seine, you are probably used to seeing booksellers with their green stalls. But have you ever heard of the first floating bookstore in Paris?

This original idea was born at the beginning of the 20th century. A book enthusiast had the brilliant idea of turning a houseboat into a bookstore. Anchored on the Seine, this bookstore offered Parisians a unique shopping experience, rocked by the waves.

Visitors could hop aboard, browse the shelves filled with books, and then sit on deck to read, while enjoying the view of the Seine. It was a real haven of peace for lovers of reading.

Today, although this first floating bookstore is no longer in operation, the idea has inspired other entrepreneurs. If you walk near the Seine, keep an eye out: you could come across one of these wonderful barges-bookstores, witnesses of a bygone era but still alive in the hearts of Parisians.

Fact 65 - The statues that speak.

Hey, curious about history! Have you ever heard of Parisian statues that "speak"? No, they don't have voices, but they tell fascinating stories if you know how to listen to them.

For centuries, Paris has been adorned with statues, each with its own history. Some commemorate historical events, others pay tribute to prominent personalities. They are silent witnesses of the evolution of the city, and if you take the time to observe them, they will whisper secrets from the past.

For example, the statue of Joan of Arc on the Place des Pyramides evokes her courage and determination. Or the statues of the Alexander III Bridge, which symbolize Franco-Russian relations. Each statue has a story to tell, an emotion to share.

Next time you walk around Paris, take a moment to stop in front of a statue. Look at her carefully, imagine her story and let yourself be carried away by the stories she could confide in you. After all, it's another way to discover the richness of Parisian history.

Fact 66 - The dancing fountains of Paris.

Hi, lover of stories and beauty! Have you ever been amazed by the dancing fountains of Paris? These aquatic masterpieces are much more than just jets of water; They are a reflection of Parisian art and culture.

For centuries, fountains have adorned the squares and gardens of Paris, offering shows of water in motion. These aquatic "dances", sometimes accompanied by plays of light, attract the eyes and captivate the imagination. They are the symbol of creativity and innovation of the City of Light.

One of the most famous is the Stravinsky Fountain, located near the Centre Pompidou. With its colorful sculptures and animated water jets, it pays tribute to the music of composer Igor Stravinsky. But this is just one example among many that dot the city.

So, during your next walk in Paris, let yourself be charmed by these dancing fountains. Take the time to sit back, watch, listen to the gentle murmur of the water and let yourself be carried away by the magic of these aquatic wonders.

Fact 67 - The rebirth of the Canal Saint-Martin.

Hey, urban adventurer! Have you ever strolled along the Canal Saint-Martin in Paris? This canal, once industrial, is now a place of relaxation and life, symbol of the transformation and urban rebirth of the capital.

Built in the early 19th century under Napoleon Bonaparte, the Canal Saint-Martin was intended to supply Paris with fresh water and facilitate the transport of goods. For a long time, he witnessed the industrial effervescence of the city, with its warehouses and bustling docks.

But over time, industrialization faded, giving way to degradation. It was only towards the end of the 20th century that the canal experienced a real renaissance. The old warehouses have been transformed into shops, cafes and art spaces. The banks, once neglected, have become popular places to walk for Parisians and tourists.

Today, the Canal Saint-Martin embodies the bohemian charm of Paris. It is a place where one can relax, picnic, or just watch the houseboats go by. A beautiful story of rebirth in the heart of the City of Light!

Fact 68 - The painters of the Seine.

Hi, art lover! Did you know that the Seine, with its reflections and its quays, has been a major source of inspiration for many artists? Yes, this iconic river has captured the imagination of famous painters, and here's why.

Since the 19th century, with the emergence of Impressionism, artists like Monet, Renoir and Pissarro have been fascinated by the changing light and scenes of everyday life along the Seine. They set their easels in the open air, capturing fleeting moments, reflections in the water and the hustle and bustle of the docks.

But it wasn't just the Impressionists. Before them, Courbet's realism and Turner's romantic vision were also influenced by the Seine. The river offered a variety of landscapes, from the tranquility of rural villages to the lively scenes of Parisian life.

Today, walking along the Seine, you can still feel this artistic atmosphere. Imagine all these great masters painting on these same banks, and be inspired by the timeless beauty of the river that has shaped so many works of art.

Fact 69 - The first school for girls.

Hey, history buff! Have you ever heard of the first school for girls? It's a fascinating story worth telling, as it marked a turning point in women's education.

In the Middle Ages, formal education was mainly reserved for boys. Girls were often educated at home, focusing on domestic skills. However, in the 17th century, in France, Saint Vincent de Paul and Louise de Marillac founded the first school for girls, offering formal education to young girls, regardless of their social status.

This initiative was revolutionary. It not only provided girls with an education, but also highlighted the importance of women's education for society. The girls learned to read, write, count, but also practical skills and Christian values.

Today, by looking back on that time, you can measure how far we've come in terms of gender equality in education. This first school for girls laid the groundwork for a movement that eventually led to universal education for all, regardless of gender.

Fact 70 - The bonfires of St. John.

Hi, lover of traditions! Have you ever witnessed the Saint-Jean bonfires in Paris? These celebrations, which take place every year on June 24, are steeped in history and symbolism.

Originally, St. John's bonfires were a pagan tradition, celebrating the summer solstice, the longest day of the year. These fires symbolized the light, warmth and power of the sun. Over time, this tradition was adopted by Christians, becoming a celebration in honor of the birth of St. John the Baptist.

In Paris, as in many other cities in France, residents gather around large fires, sing, dance and share moments of conviviality. These fires, lit in public squares, are often accompanied by festivals and processions.

Today, although the Saint-Jean bonfires have lost some of their religious significance, they remain a time of gathering and celebration, reminding Parisians and visitors of the richness of French traditions.

Fact 71 - The animals of the Vincennes Zoo.

Hey, wildlife enthusiast! Have you ever visited the Vincennes Zoo in Paris? It is an emblematic place that has seen generations of visitors, all amazed by the diversity of species it shelters.

Inaugurated in 1934, the Parc zoologique de Paris, commonly known as Vincennes Zoo, was designed as a space where animals evolve in environments close to their natural habitats. Over the years, it has undergone many renovations to adapt to modern animal welfare standards.

From African lions and Humboldt penguins to snakes and exotic birds, the zoo boasts an impressive variety of species. Each enclosure is designed to provide animals with a suitable living space, while allowing visitors to observe these magnificent creatures in optimal conditions.

If you have not yet had the opportunity to visit it, the Vincennes Zoo is a must for animal lovers. It is a real invitation to travel, without leaving the French capital!

Fact 72 - The mystery of the sundial.

Hi, lover of riddles and history! Have you ever heard of the mysterious sundials that adorn some of Paris' old buildings? These instruments, much more than just a clock, often hide fascinating stories.

Sundials, used since ancient times, make it possible to read the time thanks to the shadow cast by the sun. In Paris, many buildings are adorned with them, testifying to the importance of these objects in the daily life of past centuries. Each dial, with its inscriptions and patterns, tells a unique story.

But one of them, located in the Marais, is shrouded in mystery. It bears a strange inscription in Latin that has intrigued historians for years. Some believe it is a coded message or prophecy, while others believe it could simply be a riddle left by the artist.

The next time you walk the streets of Paris, look up and look for those sundials. Maybe you'll be the next to try to decipher their secrets!

Fact 73 - La Butte-aux-Cailles: Secret village.

Hi, urban explorer! Do you know the Butte-aux-Cailles? Nestled in the 13th arrondissement of Paris, this little corner has preserved its charm of yesteryear, far from the hustle and bustle of the Grands Boulevards.

The Butte-aux-Cailles, with its cobbled streets and low houses, looks like a village within a town. In the past, this district was known for its quarries, hence its name. Today, it is famous for its bohemian atmosphere, artists and traditional bistros.

But that's not all! The Butte-aux-Cailles also has a geological particularity. Thanks to its old quarries, spring water is naturally filtered, offering the inhabitants pure and fresh water. It is also here that the swimming pool fed by this spring water is located, a popular place for Parisians.

The next time you walk around Paris, make a detour to this neighborhood. You will discover an authentic Paris, far from tourist clichés, and let yourself be charmed by its unique atmosphere.

Fact 74 - The secrets of the Quartier des Halles.

Hey, history buff! Have you ever strolled through the Quartier des Halles in Paris? This place, in the heart of the capital, has a rich history that dates back centuries.

Originally, Les Halles was the "belly of Paris", as Émile Zola wrote. For nearly 800 years, it was the largest wholesale market in the city. Imagine, at dawn, the merchants and buyers agitating, the screams, the smells ... All of Paris came to stock up here.

But in 1971, the market was moved to Rungis, leaving behind a huge empty space. After much discussion, this void was filled by the Forum des Halles, a modern shopping centre. Above, the Nelson-Mandela Garden offers a green space in the heart of Paris.

If you walk around the neighborhood, you will still feel the soul of the old market. Cobbled streets, covered walkways and historic buildings will whisper the secrets of a bygone Paris.

Fact 75 - The yellow taxis of war.

Did you know that Parisian taxis played a crucial role during the First World War? Yes, those cars you see every day have a heroic story to tell.

In September 1914, the situation was critical for the France. German troops were advancing rapidly towards Paris. In a desperate act, the French government decided to use all possible means to strengthen the front. That's where taxis come in.

More than 600 Parisian taxis, recognizable by their yellow color, were requisitioned to quickly transport soldiers from Paris to the Battle of the Marne. These "taxis de la Marne", as they were called, transported about 6,000 soldiers in a single night.

Thanks to this rapid mobilization, French troops were able to repel the enemy and save Paris from imminent occupation. Thus, these yellow taxis, symbols of Parisian daily life, became unexpected heroes of France's history.

Fact 76 - The first public clock.

Have you ever imagined a world without a way to know the exact time at all times? This was the reality for many before the appearance of public clocks. Paris, always at the forefront of innovation, has witnessed this temporal revolution.

In the 14th century, Paris' first public clock was installed on the clock tower of the Palais de la Cité, now known as the Palais de Justice. Before that, church bells gave a rough idea of time, but nothing precise.

This clock, with its complex mechanism and large golden hand, has become a symbol of technological progress. It was not only a practical tool, but also a sign of the modernity of the city.

Today, with our watches and smartphones, it's easy to forget the importance of those early clocks. But the next time you pass by the Palais de Justice, look up and remember that time when Paris showed the world time.

Fact 77 - The musicians of the metro.

If you've ever taken the Paris metro, you've probably been greeted by the melodies of a solitary musician or an enthusiastic band. These artists, with their varied instruments, bring a touch of humanity to the underground tumult of the city.

Since the early days of the metro, musicians have seen in it a unique scene. Some seek to make themselves known, others simply play for fun or to win a few coins. Each station then becomes an improvised concert hall, where jazz, rock, classical music or ballads mingle with the sounds of the trains.

To play legally in the metro, you must obtain an authorization from the RATP. Every year, auditions are held to select the musicians. This process guarantees a certain musical quality and offers an incredible opportunity for emerging artists.

So the next time you meet a musician on the subway, take a moment to listen to him. You will participate in a Parisian tradition that has lasted for more than a century, and who knows, you might discover your next favorite melody.

Fact 78 - The harvest festival of Montmartre.

Did you know that Montmartre, despite its urban atmosphere, is home to one of the last vineyards in Paris? Every year, this little corner of greenery becomes the scene of a unique celebration: the harvest festival.

Since the 1930s, this event has celebrated the harvest of Montmartre grapes. The streets come alive, the scents of food invade the air, and local wines flow. This is an opportunity for Parisians and tourists to immerse themselves in a tradition that dates back to the time when Montmartre was still a village in its own right.

The festivities are not limited to wine tasting. Parades, concerts, art exhibitions and fireworks transform Montmartre into a real funfair. It is a manifestation of the cultural and historical richness of this emblematic district.

So, if you're in Paris in October, don't miss this celebration. You will be able to taste the wine produced on the Butte and join the party, celebrating the heritage and vitality of Montmartre.

Fact 79 - The birds of the Parisian gardens.

Have you ever taken the time to listen to the melodious songs that resonate in the gardens of Paris? These voices belong to the many birds that call the capital's green spaces home.

The Parisian gardens, despite the urban hustle and bustle, are true havens of peace for these winged creatures. From house sparrows to blackbirds to robins, these spaces provide food, shelter and nesting grounds for a variety of species.

But that's not all. Some gardens, such as the Jardin des Plantes, host rarer species, attracted by botanical diversity. There, you might have the chance to spot chickadees, finches or even kestrels flying over the alleys.

Next time you walk in a Parisian garden, look up and listen. You will be surprised by the ornithological richness that is offered to you, a reminder that nature always finds its place, even in the heart of the city.

Fact 80 - The mystery of the Conciergerie.

Have you ever heard of the Conciergerie, this historic monument located on the Ile de la Cité in Paris? Its history is as fascinating as it is mysterious.

Originally, the Conciergerie was a royal palace, the Palais de la Cité. But over time, it was turned into a prison, becoming one of the most feared places during the French Revolution. It was here that Queen Marie Antoinette was imprisoned before her execution.

The vaulted rooms and dark cells of the Conciergerie saw many prisoners, many of whom never got out. Legends tell that the souls of some still haunt the place, trying to tell their story.

When you visit the Conciergerie, you feel the weight of history. Every stone, every nook and cranny seems to whisper secrets of the past. A trip to this monument is a dive into the darkest, but also the most captivating moments of Parisian history.

Fact 81 - La Villette: Science and fun.

Did you know that Paris is home to one of the largest parks dedicated to science and culture? This is the Parc de la Villette, located in the 19th arrondissement.

This vast space, once a cattle market, was transformed into a cultural and scientific centre in 1982. It is home to the Cité des Sciences et de l'Industrie, the largest science museum in Europe. You can discover interactive exhibits, a planetarium and even a submarine!

But La Villette is not just about science. The park is also a place of relaxation and fun. With its extensive lawns, playgrounds and canals, it's a great place to relax or picnic.

The next time you're looking to combine scientific discovery with outdoor fun in Paris, think of La Villette. It is a place where learning meets entertainment, all in a green and lively setting.

Fact 82 - La Rive Droite: Chic and elegant.

Have you ever strolled on the Right Bank of the Seine in Paris? If not, you've missed out on a world of splendor and elegance. It's the beating heart of Parisian chic, where history meets glamour.

The Right Bank is famous for its wide boulevards, theatres and luxury boutiques. The Champs-Élysées, the Opera Garnier and Place Vendôme are some of the jewels. As you walk around, you will feel the sophisticated atmosphere that has seduced so many artists and writers.

But that's not all. The Right Bank is also home to lively neighborhoods like the Marais, with its narrow streets, mansions and trendy boutiques. It's a fascinating mix of old and new.

Next time you visit Paris, take the time to discover the Right Bank. Let yourself be charmed by its elegance, history and energy. It is a journey through time and fashion, in the heart of the City of Light.

Fact 83 - The secrets of the Belleville District.

Have you ever heard of Belleville? This Parisian district, perched on the heights of the city, is a true cultural melting pot, rich in history and diversity. Far from the beaten track, Belleville holds many secrets.

Historically, Belleville was a village in its own right before being annexed to Paris in the 19th century. It has long been a refuge for artists, immigrants and revolutionaries. Edith Piaf, one of the greatest French singers, was born here, and its streets have inspired many artists.

But Belleville is also a mosaic of cultures. As you wander, you'll discover bustling markets, restaurants with flavors from around the world and graffiti that turns walls into art canvases. It is a place where traditions blend and coexist harmoniously.

Next time you're in Paris, don't hesitate to explore Belleville. Behind every street corner, a secret awaits you, a story to discover. It is a journey through time and cultures, in the heart of an authentic and lively Paris.

Fact 84 - The historic bikes of Paris.

You know, Paris wasn't always the city of cars and buses. There was a time when bicycles reigned supreme on the Parisian boulevards. Let me tell you the story of bicycles in the City of Light.

At the turn of the 20th century, the bicycle became a symbol of freedom and independence. Parisians have embraced it enthusiastically, whether to get to work, to stroll or to participate in wild races. The first bike paths have even emerged, making it easier to travel on two wheels.

But with the rise of the automobile, the bicycle has gradually lost its place. It was only at the end of the 20th century, with ecological awareness, that Paris rediscovered its love for cycling. Initiatives such as the "Vélib'", a bicycle rental service, have emerged, encouraging locals and tourists to pedal again.

Today, cycling has once again become a staple of Parisian life. It testifies to the constant evolution of the city, while recalling its rich past. So next time you're in Paris, why not hop on a bike and explore the city like the Parisians of yesteryear did?

Fact 85 - The first exhibition of modern art.

Have you ever heard of the Salon des Refusés? It was in 1863, in Paris, and this event marked a decisive turning point in the history of modern art. Let me immerse you in this bubbling era of artistic innovation.

The Academy of Fine Arts, guardian of artistic traditions, organized each year the official Salon. That year, she rejected a record number of works as too avant-garde. Faced with this wave of refusal, Napoleon III decided to organize a parallel exhibition for these "refused" artists.

The Salon des Refusés exhibited works that would become emblematic, such as Manet's "Le Déjeuner sur l'herbe". These paintings, though mocked and criticized at the time, laid the foundation for modern art, defying convention and paving the way for Impressionism.

Today, these works are celebrated and worth fortunes. They remind us that innovation and breaking with the past can be misunderstood in their time, but that they can also redefine the future. So the next time you visit a modern art museum, remember those bold artists who dared to challenge the status quo.

Fact 86 - Street festivals in Paris.

Paris, the City of Light, is not only famous for its monuments and history. Have you ever heard of its street festivals? These events transform the capital into a lively stage, where every street corner resonates with music, dance and colour.

One of the most emblematic is the Fête de la Musique, celebrated on June 21. Since 1982, amateur and professional musicians have been invading the streets, parks and cafes to share their passion. From jazz to rock to classical music, there is something for everyone.

The Paris Carnival, a tradition that dates back to the Middle Ages, is another major celebration. Every year, thousands of people march in colorful costumes, dancing and singing to the rhythm of brass bands.

Finally, let's not forget the Nuit Blanche, an October night when art takes possession of the city. Installations, performances and ephemeral exhibitions transform Paris into an open-air museum. So, if you have the opportunity, immerse yourself in one of these festivals and feel the unique energy of Paris en fête!

Fact 87 - The animals of the Menagerie.

Have you ever heard of the Ménagerie du Jardin des Plantes in Paris? It is one of the oldest zoos in the world, founded in 1794, and it has played a crucial role in the preservation and study of animal species.

Over the years, this place has hosted exotic and rare animals, such as the first giraffe in France in 1827. This giraffe, offered to King Charles X by the viceroy of Egypt, has become a real celebrity, attracting thousands of curious people.

The Menagerie was also a place of scientific discovery. Researchers have studied the behaviour and biology of many species, contributing to modern conservation science.

Today, although more modest in size compared to large modern zoos, the Menagerie remains an iconic place. It is home to more than 1,200 animals, some of which are endangered. If you are walking around Paris, do not hesitate to visit this historic place and immerse yourself in the fascinating world of its feathered, hairy and scaled residents.

Fact 88 - The mystery of the rue des Chantres.

Have you ever strolled through the Latin Quarter of Paris? If so, you may have crossed the discreet rue des Chantres. Nestled behind the majestic Notre-Dame Cathedral, this narrow alley holds mysteries dating back to the Middle Ages.

Originally, the rue des Chantres was the vibrant heart of Parisian religious life. It took its name from the cantors of the cathedral, those men of faith who raised their voices in sacred songs. They lived and studied here, in houses that lined the street.

But legend also tells that the street was the scene of strange events. Melodious and mysterious songs resounded some evenings, without anyone being able to identify their origin. Some said it was the work of the spirits of the deceased cantors, still attached to their former home.

Today, the Rue des Chantres is peaceful, but its mysterious past continues to fascinate. If you are in Paris, take the time to browse it and imagine the echoes of past voices that could still resonate there.

Fact 89 - The Mouzaïa district: Little treasure.

Have you ever heard of the Mouzaïa district in Paris? Located in the 19th arrondissement, far from the beaten tourist track, this district is a real hidden gem of the capital.

Originally, the Mouzaïa was a gypsum quarry. After its exploitation, the land was transformed into a set of small houses with gardens, often called "workers' houses". These houses, built at the beginning of the 20th century, offer a picturesque charm with their colorful facades and flower gardens.

What makes this neighborhood so special is its peaceful, almost village-like atmosphere, right in the heart of the noisy metropolis. Walking through its narrow streets, you could almost forget that you are in Paris, as the change of scenery is total.

If you are looking for a corner of tranquility away from the hustle and bustle of Paris, La Mouzaïa is the ideal place. A walk there will transport you to another world, where time seems to have stopped.

Fact 90 - The secrets of the Bercy district.

Do you really know the Bercy district in Paris? Located in the 12th arrondissement, Bercy is steeped in history and full of secrets unknown to the general public.

In the past, Bercy was the largest wine market in the world. In the 19th century, thousands of barrels of wine passed through its warehouses every day. As you walk, you can still see the old rails that were used to transport these barrels and the original cobblestones that bear witness to this bygone era.

Today, the neighborhood has changed a lot. The old warehouses have been transformed into shops, restaurants and cinemas, forming the famous "Bercy Village". But that's not all: the Parc de Bercy, with its thematic gardens, is a haven of peace in the heart of the city.

So, the next time you go to Bercy, take a moment to explore its alleys and discover the traces of its winemaking past. You will be surprised by the treasures that this neighborhood has to offer.

Fact 91 - The vintage cars of Paris.

Have you ever dreamed of travelling back in time while walking through the streets of Paris? The vintage cars that still crisscross the capital allow you to do it, at least in imagination.

At the beginning of the 20th century, Paris saw the arrival of the first automobiles. These vehicles, with their elegant shapes and purring engines, were the symbol of luxury and modernity. Brands like Citroën, Peugeot and Renault marked this era, producing iconic models that are now sought after by collectors.

Every year, events such as the "Traversée de Paris" allow you to admire these vehicles of yesteryear. Hundreds of vintage cars, motorcycles and bicycles roam the city, offering a timeless spectacle.

So the next time you come across one of these wonders on four wheels, take a moment to admire it. These cars bear witness to a bygone era, but they continue to make the heart of Paris beat to the rhythm of their engine.

Fact 92 - The first Parisian radio station.

Have you ever imagined a world without the ability to turn on the radio and instantly listen to music, news or shows? For Paris, this revolution began in the 1920s.

The first Parisian radio station, Radiola, began broadcasting in 1922. It was a time when technology was still in its infancy, and the idea of transmitting voice and music over the airwaves was almost magical. Parisians quickly became passionate about this new medium, gathering around radio sets to listen to news bulletins, plays and concerts.

Over time, radio became a central part of Parisian culture. Iconic broadcasts have emerged, and famous voices have marked the airwaves, creating a unique connection between listeners and the city.

Today, even in the digital age, radio holds a special place in the hearts of Parisians. It recalls a time when, for the first time, the sounds of the city could be shared, live, with all its inhabitants.

Fact 93 - The artists of the Pont des Arts.

Do you remember the last time you crossed the Pont des Arts in Paris? This pedestrian bridge, linking the Institut de France to the Louvre, is much more than just a footbridge over the Seine.

For decades, the Pont des Arts has been a favorite place for artists. Painters, musicians, poets and dancers come here to be inspired by the beauty of Paris and share their art with passers-by. The atmosphere is unique, lulled by the melodies of the guitars and the bright colors of the paintings in progress.

But it is not only a place of artistic expression. It is also a place where Parisians and tourists come to relax, enjoy the view and, sometimes, leave a trace of their passage. You may have heard of the tradition of "love padlocks", even though this practice was banned in 2015 to preserve the structure of the bridge.

Today, the Pont des Arts remains a vibrant symbol of Parisian cultural life, a space where art and love meet in the heart of the city.

Fact 94 - The festival of lights of Paris.

Have you ever had the chance to walk the streets of Paris during the Festival of Lights? If not, let me transport you to this magical event that illuminates the City of Light every year.

Historically, Paris has always been associated with light, hence its nickname. But during the Festival of Lights, this name takes on its full meaning. Artistic and innovative light installations adorn monuments, parks and streets, transforming the city into a real tableau vivant.

This is not simply a demonstration of technical prowess. It is a celebration of art, culture and innovation. Each installation tells a story, evokes an emotion or highlights a particular aspect of the city. Artists from all over the world come to participate, bringing with them new perspectives and ideas.

So, if you are in Paris during this period, do not hesitate to let yourself be guided by the lights. It is a unique experience that will allow you to rediscover the capital in a totally new light.

Fact 95 - The butterflies of the Jardin des Plantes.

Have you ever felt the magic of seeing a butterfly delicately land on a flower? At the Jardin des Plantes in Paris, this magic is multiplied by a thousand, offering an unforgettable natural spectacle.

For years, the Jardin des Plantes has housed a greenhouse dedicated to tropical butterflies. In this warm and humid oasis, hundreds of butterflies of all sizes and colors twirl freely, creating a fascinating aerial ballet. These delicate creatures come from various parts of the world, offering incredible diversity in one place.

But it's not just a show. The greenhouse plays an educational role, raising visitors' awareness of the beauty of nature and the importance of biodiversity. It also highlights the threats to these insects, including the destruction of their natural habitat.

Next time you visit Paris, take a moment to lose yourself among these winged wonders. It is a soothing and enriching experience, reminding you of the fragile and ephemeral beauty of nature.

Fact 96 - The Square des Missions-Étrangères.

Have you ever heard of the Square des Missions-Étrangères, nestled in the heart of the 7th arrondissement of Paris? This little corner of greenery hides a rich and fascinating history.

Originally, this land belonged to the Society of Foreign Missions of Paris, a Catholic organization founded in the seventeenth century. Its mission was to send priests to Asia to evangelize. The square was then part of their vast estate, including a chapel and a seminary.

But what makes this place really intriguing is the presence of an obelisk in its center. Erected in 1867, it pays tribute to the missionaries martyred in Korea. The names of these men of faith are engraved on the stone, recalling their sacrifice.

Today, the square is a haven of peace for residents and tourists. But as you walk between its alleys, do not forget to stop for a moment in front of this obelisk, silent witness of a bygone era and boundless dedication.

Fact 97 - Le Quartier de Batignolles : Discreet charm.

Have you ever strolled through the Batignolles district, located in the 17th arrondissement of Paris? This place, once a village in its own right, exudes a unique atmosphere, mixing history and modernity.

In the nineteenth century, the Batignolles were the haunt of artists and writers, attracted by its bohemian atmosphere. Manet, Degas and even the poet Paul Verlaine left their mark there. The small cobbled streets and artists' studios still bear witness to this flourishing era.

But Batignolles is also a green setting in the heart of Paris. The Square des Batignolles, with its pond and tall trees, is a favorite place for families and nature lovers. More recently, Martin Luther King Park was born, offering a modern and playful space.

If you are looking for a corner of Paris away from the tourist hustle and bustle, Batignolles is a destination of choice. Between its cafes, independent shops and green spaces, this district will charm you with its discretion and authenticity.

Fact 98 - The secrets of the Quartier de la Chapelle.

Do you know the Quartier de la Chapelle, nestled in the 18th arrondissement of Paris? It is a vibrant place, rich in history and diversity, with many secrets.

Historically, the Chapel was a small village outside the walls of Paris. Over the centuries, it has integrated into the city, but has retained its distinct charm. It was here that Joan of Arc was arrested in 1431, a fact often forgotten by many.

The neighborhood is also a crossroads of cultures. As you walk, you will discover the "Little Jaffna", the heart of the Tamil community of Paris. The streets are full of shops selling exotic spices, colorful saris and culinary specialties.

But La Chapelle is also the direct urban evolution. With the recent transformation of the Halle Pajol into an ecological youth hostel and cultural space, the district is showing its modern face. If you are looking for a mix of history, culture and innovation, the Chapel awaits you with its well-kept secrets.

Fact 99 - The airships of Paris.

Have you ever imagined the sky of Paris crisscrossed by huge airships? At the turn of the 20th century, it was a fascinating reality and a technological feat.

The first balloon flight took place in 1783, but it was at the beginning of the 20th century that airships really took off. These giants of the air were used for travel, observations and even military missions during the First World War.

One of the most iconic sites associated with airships is the Parc des Princes. Before being the stadium you know today, it was a landing ground for these machines. Imagine, a majestic airship descending gently to the ground, under the amazed eyes of Parisians.

Unfortunately, after several notable accidents, including the Hindenburg tragedy in 1937, the airship era came to an end. But their legacy remains, reminiscent of a time when the Parisian sky was the scene of daring and innovative aerial adventures.

Fact 100 - The first children's bookstore.

Did you know that Paris is home to the first bookstore entirely dedicated to children? Yes, before that, children's books were often relegated to an obscure corner of general bookstores.

The "Librairie des Enfants" opened its doors in 1933, founded by Adrienne Monnier. Located in the heart of the Latin Quarter, this bookstore revolutionized the way children's books were perceived, putting them at the forefront of the literary scene.

Adrienne was a firm believer in the importance of children's literature. She wanted children to have a space of their own, where they could explore, dream and educate themselves through the pages. Thanks to her, generations of Parisian children have discovered the pleasure of reading.

Today, although the original bookstore no longer exists, its spirit lives on. Paris is full of bookstores dedicated to young people, testifying to the importance of cultivating a love of books from an early age.

Conclusion

After walking through the winding streets, grandiose monuments and hidden corners of Paris through these 100 facts, one thing is clear: Paris is a city of immeasurable wealth, where every stone and alley has a story to tell. It is an intoxicating blend of past and present, art and science, dream and reality.

But beyond the facts and anecdotes, what we must remember is the spirit of Paris. A spirit of innovation, resilience, love and passion. A city that, despite hardships and centuries, has never lost its brilliance or charm. It continues to inspire artists, writers, dreamers and travelers around the world.

As you close this book, I hope you will take with you not only new knowledge, but also a renewed love for this magical city. Because, as Victor Hugo said so well: "Breathing Paris preserves the soul." May these incredible facts inspire you to explore, dream and cherish Paris, today and always.

Marc Dresgui

Quiz

1) What animal was NOT present at the Jardin des Plantes?

    a) Lion
    b) Kangaroo
    c) Dinosaur
    d) Bear

2) Which bridge is the oldest bridge in Paris?

    a) Alexander III Bridge
    b) New Bridge
    c) Pont des Arts
    d) Alma Bridge

3) Which Parisian school is more than 800 years old?

    a) The École normale supérieure
    b) École Polytechnique
    c) The Sorbonne
    d) HEC Paris

4) Which Parisian monument is nicknamed "A glass jewel"?

    a) The Eiffel Tower
    b) The Louvre
    c) The Grand Palais

d) The Philharmonie de Paris

5) **Who is the author of "Les Misérables"?**
   a) Emile Zola
   b) Marcel Proust
   c) Victor Hugo
   d) Alexandre Dumas

6) **Where does the Fête de la Musique take place?**
   a) In schools
   b) In theatres
   c) In stadiums
   d) In the streets

7) **What is the name of the famous cabaret with French Cancan dancers?**
   a) The Crazy Horse
   b) The Moulin Rouge
   c) The Olympia
   d) The Lido

8) **In which Parisian cemetery are ghosts said to be lurking?**
   a) Montparnasse Cemetery
   b) Père Lachaise Cemetery

c) Passy Cemetery
d) Montmartre Cemetery

9) **Which river has already frozen in Paris?**
   a) The Rhône
   b) The Loire
   c) The Seine
   d) The Rhine

10) **Which artist is associated with life in color in Montmartre?**
    a) Vincent van Gogh
    b) Toulouse-Lautrec
    c) Pablo Picasso
    d) Claude Monet

11) **Before the Revolution, what did the Bastille represent?**
    a) A public square
    b) A prison
    c) A royal palace
    d) A market

12) **Where is the Historic Menagerie?**
    a) Bois de Boulogne

- b) Belleville Park
- c) Jardin des Plantes
- d) Buttes-Chaumont Park

13) Which neighborhood is known for its discreet charm?

- a) Swamp
- b) Batignolles
- c) Saint-Germain
- d) Belleville

14) What means of transport was popular in Paris before cars?

- a) Trams
- b) Tuk-tuks
- c) Rickshaws
- d) Trolleys

15) Which specific school was created in the 17th century?

- a) Lycée Louis-le-Grand
- b) Lycée Henri-IV
- c) Lycée Montaigne
- d) A girls-only school

16) Where does the harvest festival take place each year?

    a) Latin Quarter
    b) Montmartre
    c) Belleville
    d) Batignolles

17) Which neighborhood is known for its street festivals?

    a) The Marais
    b) Saint-Germain
    c) Bercy
    d) La Villette

18) Which Parisian monument houses the great men of the nation?

    a) The Arc de Triomphe
    b) The Pantheon
    c) The Eiffel Tower
    d) The Louvre

19) Where can I find artists exhibiting their work outdoors?

    a) On the Pont des Arts
    b) Place du Tertre

c) Rue de Rivoli
d) On the banks of the Seine

20) What innovation was presented at the Universal Exhibition in Paris?

   a) The steam engine
   b) The light bulb
   c) The Eiffel Tower
   d) The phone

Answers

1) What animal was NOT present at the Jardin des Plantes?

Correct answer: c) Dinosaur

2) Which bridge is the oldest bridge in Paris?

Correct answer: b) Pont Neuf

3) Which Parisian school is more than 800 years old?

Correct answer: c) The Sorbonne

4) **Which Parisian monument is nicknamed "A glass jewel"?**

    Correct answer: c)The Grand Palais

5) **Who is the author of "Les Misérables"?**

    Correct answer: c)Victor Hugo

6) **Where does the Fête de la Musique take place?**

    Correct answer: (d)On the streets

7) **What is the name of the famous cabaret with French Cancan dancers?**

    Correct answer: b)The Moulin Rouge

8) **In which Parisian cemetery are ghosts said to be lurking?**

    Correct answer: b)Père Lachaise Cemetery

9) **Which river has already frozen in Paris?**

    Correct answer: c)The Seine

10) Which artist is associated with life in color in Montmartre?

Correct answer: b) Toulouse-Lautrec

11) Before the Revolution, what did the Bastille represent?

Correct answer: (b) A prison

12) Where is the Historic Menagerie?

Correct answer: c) Jardin des Plantes

13) Which neighborhood is known for its discreet charm?

Correct answer: b) Batignolles

14) What means of transport was popular in Paris before cars?

Correct answer: a) Trams

15) Which specific school was created in the 17th century?

Correct answer: (d) A girls-only school

16) Where does the harvest festival take place each year?

Correct answer: b) Montmartre

17) Which neighborhood is known for its street festivals?

Correct answer: c) Bercy

18) Which Parisian monument houses the great men of the nation?

Correct answer: b) The Pantheon

19) Where can I find artists exhibiting their work outdoors?

Correct answer: b) Place du Tertre

20) What innovation was presented at the Universal Exhibition in Paris?

Correct answer: c) The Eiffel Tower

Printed in Great Britain
by Amazon